Young Adult's
Guide to a
Business Career

Young Adult's Guide to a Business Career

M. J. Giles

Business Books, LLC
EVANSVILLE, INDIANA

First printing 2004

ISBN 0-9723714-3-5
LCCN 2002115500

ATTENTION CORPORATIONS, UNIVERSITIES, COLLEGES, AND PROFESSIONAL ORGANIZATIONS: Quantity discounts are available on bulk purchases of this book for educational, gift purposes, or as premiums for increasing magazine subscriptions or renewals. Special books or book excerpts can also be created to fit specific needs. For information, please contact Business Books, LLC, 2709 Washington Avenue, 21A, Evansville, IN 47714, (812) 471-7924.

To my parents, Bekki and Jay Giles,
I love you two.
—M. J. G.

TABLE OF CONTENTS

ACKNOWLEDGMENTS

I am grateful to the impressive group of individuals whose expertise was extremely helpful as well as encouraging throughout the writing of this book. These include Dr. Joy Pelluchette, professor of management at the University of Southern Indiana, for her assistance in answering questions regarding my choices of careers in management. Jamie Wicks, a trust officer for Fifth Third Bank, was very helpful in my quest for knowledge in the area of trusts as well as other financial careers such as the career of the financial advisor.

Harry Lukens, an insurance agent for Jesse F. Stock Insurance Company, was helpful with his insight into a career in insurance. Harry has been in the business of insurance since his father opened his own business over 46 years ago. Corey Ainscough, a computer technician with Old National Bank, was very informative in the area of computers, particularly in his own profession as a computer technician.

Jeffrey Williamson received his master's degree in accountancy from the University of Southern Indiana. Jeffrey is currently employed with C.S. Oates Accountancy Corporation as a staff accountant and was an excellent source of information within the area of accounting and finance. Jeff May is currently employed with Regency Commercial Associates and was very resourceful and insightful into his career as a manager. He is a property manager and holds a bachelor's degree with a major in finance. Matthew May is currently employed with WFIE Channel 14 and is certified as a computer network technician with an outstanding knowledge base for his passion, computers.

Kim Louden was an excellent source of information. She holds a bachelor's degree with a major in economics and is currently employed as a credit analyst with Old National Bank. Shawn Graham holds a bachelor's degree with a double major in both mathematics and economics and has passed the first actuarial exam. He is currently employed with American General Finance and was informative in the actuarial science area.

Again, I would like to give special thanks to all of these people for helping to keep the information in this book accurate and up to date.

INTRODUCTION

In today's world, where change is the norm, it is hard to figure out exactly what we want to do with the rest of our lives. There is so much opportunity and so many ways to achieve what we want in life that transforming complexity into simplicity becomes the key to understanding our future. In order to figure out exactly what it is you want to do with the rest of your life, it is crucial to put off making a final decision until it is absolutely necessary. Never keep a closed mind about any career path. Promise yourself that you are going to explore every option you find interesting—and even some of the options you do not find interesting. When you make a decision about the rest of your life, there is so much excitement you become narrowly focused on just that career idea. Make sure that when you make a choice, it is the right one for you—not for someone else.

Throughout this book, I try to point out the advantages and disadvantages of many different careers to ensure that you understand that with any career, there are negative sides as well as positive sides. When we find a career we enjoy, we tend to focus on the positive aspects of it, often overlooking the negatives. For ex-

1

ample, many younger finance-focused individuals want to be financial advisors. In their mind, the role of the financial advisor is simply to sit on the phone all day wheeling and dealing in the stock market making all kinds of money. This is not true for any stage of the financial advisor's career. Actually, the first five years as a financial advisor are some of the most important years of any financial advisor's career. There is so much rejection that must be accepted constructively, that if the financial advisor takes these rejections personally, it can completely destroy his or her goals and dreams.

Between chapters there are four topics that should be considered important in your life. In fact, if you are in high school or a freshman or sophomore in college, these individual sections of the book are probably the most important sections for you to read. As a young adult, it is crucial to your future to gain all of the experience possible and meet with as many professional people as you can during your college years.

More and more employers reviewing resumes are looking for real-world experience over the typical four-year college degree. Also, in many cases, it is not just what you know that will get you a job, but also who you know. Once you have the experience and meet the individuals who will be crucial to your career, displaying your knowledge through your resume and during your interview are the two main tools that you have to convince your prospective employers you are qualified and capable of performing in the position for which you have applied.

Don't stop with this book; get the opinions of others until you can develop a style you feel comfortable with. There is not just one way to write a resume or to perform during an interview. Determine what your style is, and then perfect it!

It is my hope this book will not only give you a brief introduction into the careers that might be of interest to you, but will ensure that you realize there are opportunities everywhere you look. Do not limit yourself to what you think is right, because often it is the opportunities you do not know about that can bring you the most success and happiness.

Computers

CHAPTER 1

COMPUTER PROGRAMMER

In today's society, we have become completely dependent on computers. The computer programmer is responsible for providing programs to run everything from the simplicity of a treadmill to the complexity of sending our men to the moon. We owe much of the growth of modern society to the computer programmer. If it were not for the programmer, our economy would be growing at an incredibly slower rate.

CAREER PROFILE
Entry salary range: $30,000 to $38,000
Prerequisites: Bachelor's degree including some extra courses in business for application reasons
Employers: Banks, manufacturing corporations, hospitals, colleges, etc.
Websites for Review: www.iscet.org (International Society of Certified Electronics Technicians)   www.iccp.org (Institute for Certification of Computing Professionals)   www.acm.org (Association for Computing Machinery)

The career for the computer programmer is so broad, it is extremely hard to determine exactly what a programmer does. A programmer may write programs for games, company systems, cell phones, airplanes, motor vehicles, or satellites that float thousands of miles above our heads. The programmer tells a computer what outputs to produce given certain inputs into the system.

It is becoming more and more evident that the role of a programmer requires a great deal of patience and attention to details. A programmer must have patience because when a problem occurs, it may take minutes, hours, or even days to correct it. Also, this one problem may be as simple as one wrong code or a mistyped word that the computer is unable to catch. The role of a computer programmer requires paying close attention to all of the details within every program written or maintained.

Disadvantages

As technology improves, the programs become much more complex, causing your job to become more hectic as the years continue. It is important to keep up with all of the new technology because if you fall behind, then a younger programmer right out of college may take your job. It is critical that you dedicate a lot of time to this position as well. Frequently, computer programmers work on weekends and evenings, depending on what problems may have come about during the business day.

Another disadvantage is that you are always on call. If you are on the 8th hole of the state championship tournament and that pager vibrates in your pocket, it is time to put the golf clubs in the trunk and get back to the office. You'll need to maintain a flexible schedule if you intend to pursue the career of a computer programmer.

Advantages

As a computer programmer, you will have job security because it is you who will continue America's growth into the upcoming years, as long as you keep up with the latest technology. Some computer programmers are also allowed to make their own schedules if they commit to certain hours. Although your employer may keep you on a short leash, some computer programmers may be able to get away with a lot of stuff that other employees cannot.

Coming and going as you please is a major luxury for many computer programmers. In many circumstances, a computer programmer's services are not always needed but, when they are needed, it is extremely crucial that they execute their objective very quickly.

COMPUTER TECHNICIAN

There are two main types of computer technician careers. The first computer technician works for a company fixing the computers the company sells, solving all sorts of problems from hardware to software. Many individuals who have a personal computer may find it difficult to operate their computer and when something goes wrong, it is up to this technician to solve the problem.

The other type of computer technician is employed by a specific company to work exclusively on their computers. Most companies have their computers running on a network and these networks will crash from time to time. Generally, it is the network administrator who will get you back on your feet, but the computer technician is usually responsible for getting the computers back up and running in a short amount of time as well.

CAREER PROFILE
Entry salary range: $19,000 to $22,000
Prerequisites: Associate degree in a computer-related field is the bare minimum
Employers: Computer retailers, computer manufacturers, banks, and hospitals
Websites for Review: www.iccp.org (Institute for Certification of Computing Professionals) www.eta-sda.com (Electronics Technicians Association and Satellite Dealers Association)

It is typical of a computer to run for years, and then for no good reason, just never start back up because of a bad motherboard or other part of the system. The computer technician has the responsibility of fixing this computer in as brief an amount of time as possible. The technician is also responsible for installations through system conversions, upgrading the software or the hardware such as new memory chips or a new central processing unit (CPU).

In today's world, more and more people are dependent on their computers. When that computer crashes, or will not operate the way it should, it is time for the computer technician to be a hero and get the computer back and running as quickly as possible. For a computer technician, patience and understanding are two important skills. These individuals work a lot of overtime and try to explain the complexities of the computer to individuals who lack the experience required to run them efficiently. A computer technician must have patience and understanding with the individuals who perform their daily functions on the computer. The computer technician should simply refer to these people as job security.

This career is becoming more and more demanded by college graduates. In today's economy, you are going to have to find ways to separate you from your peers. These could include becoming active in computer clubs at your school or meeting people in the computer field. Networking in this career, as with most careers, will help you get a head start in this profession. Also, becoming certified in Microsoft, Novell, or CISCO can separate you from your peers. These certifications can be self-taught and can also be attained as early as high school if you are a self-motivated individual.

Disadvantages

If you truly love your job as a computer technician, there are not many disadvantages to this career. It can be frustrating at times when the new software your company has decided to use does not communicate with the current software or hardware your company currently may have. Also, if your company undergoes a major conversion or system change, you may find it frustrating to deal with such a large project and its complications. If you are a people person with patience and a need to work with computers, you will find it difficult to be upset with your choice of this career.

Advantages

As a computer technician you will meet new people and make new friendships almost every day. You will find yourself dealing with people from within the company in nearly all departments. Having the chance to meet these people is great and knowing they need you is rewarding. When their computer goes down, you are in demand. Also, this is not a career that you learn how to do, and then stop learning. In our technological society, companies will send you to continuing education classes, all paid for by the company, and will require you to learn all of the new and upcoming technological advances. If you are intrigued by computers, this career is probably one of the most exciting of all.

One of the greatest advantages is that no one will require you to sit in a cubicle all day and work on projects or do the same thing each and every day. There are new things that must be taken care of on a day-today basis. Unlike the computer programmer, there is little repetition in this career. Most days, when you walk into the office, you will have no clue as to what it is you will be doing that day. The demand for the computer technician with an interest in meeting new people will continue to be high as technology continues to grow.

WEBMASTER

We have all been to websites—both good and bad. Ebay, for instance, is a well-done, popular site. Who designs these web pages and maintains them?

A webmaster creates sites for companies who want to expand their business domestically or internationally. He or she is responsible for the content, functions, and design of the web page. It is the webmaster who has to understand what attracts individuals to visit a website and stay for a while to browse all of the content or products that site has to offer.

CAREER PROFILE
Entry salary range: $25,000 to $29,000
Prerequisites: Bachelor's degree
Employers: Department stores, web-based companies, hotels, restaurants, etc.
Websites for Review: www.association.org/index.html (Association of Internet Professionals)   www.iwanet.org (International Webmasters Association)

Having an artistic and creative mind is essential for success in this career. Using colors, shapes, pictures, and any other visual affects to entice the viewer is the main priority for the webmaster. In the beginning, websites were black and white with no pictures. There were only words because neither the Internet nor technology was developed enough to show any type of graphics. Today it is crucial for the webmaster to have a good understanding as to what attracts different people, what makes an individual want to buy products or continue browsing the website. They have to understand what makes a website good or bad.

In the beginning all websites were designed using HTML—Hypertext Markup Language—which was a complicated language that had to be learned to be successful. In the last couple of years, there have been many programs such as Microsoft FrontPage to help the webmaster build websites. With FrontPage, you can simply cut and paste to design a web page and the program will write most all of the HTML for you. These programs save the webmaster a lot of time and prevent errors. Understanding HTML, along with many other programs, is still demanded from your employer because changes to the program will be made and you will be expected to rewrite the HTML program.

Disadvantages

Larger companies such as Microsoft, Yahoo, and Ebay have such large websites, many things such as errors and omissions can be overlooked. Although the complexity of these websites has been greatly reduced because of more sophisticated software, understanding the advertising and goals of your web page can be a bit much for one individual. In this case, the webmaster position is more likely to be done by a team of webmasters. Imagine the job of webmaster for Ebay, trying to maintain all of the advertisements, selling items and links within the site as well as those that lead outside of it.

Also, working with web pages can be frustrating. Dealing with color schemes, the size of windows, graphics, and the speed of your web page's loading times can be frustrating. Most people will only wait a couple of seconds for a web page to load; if it takes too long, they will simply move on to another website.

Advantages

Because computers—especially home computers—have become so common, websites are being used by individuals for buying securities and insurance, reviewing their online banking accounts, shopping, and many other things, which ensures that the number of jobs for webmasters will grow.

As a webmaster, it is your responsibility to make sure your website is as appealing as possible. If you enjoy working with computers, being creative, and working with web pages that will please your viewers, a career as a webmaster may be just right for you.

NETWORK TECHNICIAN

Virtually everyone uses networks in our society. We are extremely dependent on computers and the networks that connect them. A network can be defined as two or more computers linked together sharing information. Networks connect large or small companies; all of the banks in the world, and people to each other. Almost every cellular phone that we use today is connected to a network. A network technician is an entry-level career for an individual right out of college who has an interest and knowledge in this area of computers. It is the lead-in career to becoming a network administrator. Network technicians form the foundation for every network we use today.

CAREER PROFILE
Entry salary range: $21,000 to $25,000
Prerequisites: A two-year associate degree is the minimum but most organizations are now requiring a bachelor's degree and certifications
Employers: Banks, cellular companies, libraries, the government, TV and radio stations
Websites for Review: www.ibm.com/education/certify/news/peridc.htm www.npanet.org (Networking Professional Association) www.comptia.com

Basically, a network technician is in charge of the maintenance and the proper upkeep of the network. A network technician could be responsible for work as simple as backing up current jobs and cleaning up the server, as difficult as configuring the two computers and making them work together through a device called a hub, or ensuring there is a large enough supercomputer to run the network of computers. When working on a network, computers have a problem with crashing. When a network completely crashes, it is the computer technician who must decipher the problem and get it back up and running. When you are dealing with business, time is money. Just because your computer stops working, does not mean time is going to wait for you to catch up so you must learn to be efficient and fast.

Another function of the network technician is to oversee every individual who uses the server. An event log will tell you the time and the user who may have violated the rules or tried to do something illegal. Technicians use a "firewall" to help them ensure no one on the inside is doing anything wrong and no one on the outside is not trying to get inside. This is a security system to protect the company's computers as well as the company's private information. Although it is illegal for someone to break through the firewall, when a hacker finds his or her way through your system, they can create a major headache for you and your firm.

Disadvantages

The network technician is primarily responsible for the network's functioning. When this network fails to work as it should, your phone will ring off the hook. People will likely be upset if failure happens frequently. When a bank manager needs to finish a report for some clients who are coming in, and the network is down, his or her frustrations will be taken out on the network technician.

A major disadvantage, as with most all computer-related jobs, is that new technology continues to come out and you must stay on top of things. As you get older, college graduates stay the same age and they continue to get smarter and smarter. You must stay up-to-date with new technology.

Advantages

The network technician is in high demand. When computers are not working the way they should be or the network has completely shut down, it is time to prove your magic. Whip out all of your education and experience and make something good happen. Network technicians take a lot of heat when things go wrong, but in reality almost everyone loves the technician because without him or her, the company would be in big trouble when its computers do not communicate well with one another.

If you really enjoy working with computers, this career is perfect for you because you get the chance to work with the hardware as well as the application side of the computer. The discovery and advancement of networks have revolutionized the way we conduct relationships in our personal lives as well as in business. The use of networks will continue to enrich our lives with the ability to keep in touch with the world in the click of a button.

SYSTEMS ANALYST

Systems analysts find themselves visiting potential clients to pick apart their current computer hardware as well as their software and letting them know what they could do to make their computers run more effectively and efficiently. Imagine what it would be like to visit the upper management of a corporation that has been using the same software for 10 years and try to convince them your software can revolutionize the way they do business. Sometimes a company needs its entire computer network upgraded, costing thousands of dollars in new hardware. Even in this situation, a true systems analyst would simply say, "It's all in a day's work!"

CAREER PROFILE
Entry salary range: $23,000 to $29,000
Prerequisites: Bachelor's degree
Employers: Banks, brokerage clearing firms, consulting firms, and firms such as Microsoft and Sun Microsystems
Websites for Review: www.qai.org (Quality Assurance Institute) www.ieee.org (Institute of Electrical and Electronics Engineers) www.acm.org (Association for Computing Machinery)

One strategy a systems analyst can use is finding synergies within a company. Computers simplify complicated things so when synergies are found, the persuasion to switch to a new computer system is relatively easy. Synergy can be defined as 1 + 1 = 3. For example, if a company can combine two procedures, it

18

can eliminate a position within the firm, which will eventually save enough money to pay for the new system the analyst is trying to sell. After the negotiation is done and the systems analyst has convinced upper management his or her system will benefit the company, it is now time to figure out exactly what the company needs to tweak the system to work more efficiently.

Since virtually every business is run differently, one computer system cannot be designed for every company. The base of the computer system may always remain, but adjustments must be made to ensure the system will work well to provide the output they are looking for. In order to find out exactly what needs to be done, the analyst will sit down with several managers as well as several entry-level employees to find out exactly what they do and what they need the computers to do.

A systems analyst must have a good understanding of hardware, software, programming, and networking. Basically, the systems analyst must be just short of a computer genius so when problems arise, he or she has an understanding of how to correct them.

Disadvantages

This career is challenging and requires talented individuals who not only work well with their heads, but must also be good with their hands. It is demanding and may require quite a bit of traveling as well as long hours. Just as the computer programmer, one does not start a complicated computer program and end it in one sitting. Problems arise for several years and must be tweaked to make the system bug-free.

This career also involves sales and persuasion. Having a good understanding of psychology and the way people react in different situations is crucial if you are going to be successful as a systems analyst. When dealing with those resistant to change, you are likely to encounter rejection. Having the ability to deal with it and move on is important. Working as a systems analyst will be easier if you are knowledgeable about your software.

Advantages

If you are lucky enough to be one of these multi-talented individuals, you will have no problem finding success in your career. Demand will likely be high for the next several years. In fact, the systems analyst is currently among one of the fastest-growing occupations today.

Unlike the computer programmer, you are not stuck in a cubicle all day working on the same computer. The systems analyst will work with people and interact with them every day. The systems analyst gets hands-on experience with several different aspects of the computer. The computer programmer programs computers and the webmaster designs web pages. But the systems analyst will program computers, set up networks, configure hardware, and debug any problem that may arise within the software the company provides. With all of this excitement, it is hard to imagine finding a job in the computer field other than systems analyst that can meet the needs of an individual who enjoys working with computers.

Internships and Co-ops

The most—and I repeat, *the most*—important thing a students can do to better prepare themselves for the world after school, is to find on-the-job training through the use of internships and co-ops. Whether these opportunities are paid or unpaid, they are important to your success as soon as you enter the world of full-time employment.

An internship is typically on-the-job training for which you receive little pay or even no pay. In essence, it is a free education drawn from your experiences and hard work within that corporation. Usually completed at the same time you are attending school, internships ordinarily require a couple hours a day and tend to work around your classes so graduation is not postponed.

A co-op is exactly the opposite. Generally, you attend school for one semester and then work for one semester. Co-ops are usually all paid and provide you with a feeling of what the real world is truly like. Co-ops offer full-time employment and give you the chance to gain experience in a job while being supervised by a professional in that area.

Both internships and co-ops are great opportunities to achieve great things. Moreover, they are awesome resume builders.

There are many ways to go about getting an internship. Networking with individuals and asking if they know of any internships within their organization is a great way to find out about internships in your area. Do not be afraid to pick up the phone and call someone in a department of a company in which you are interested. Nothing will show your interest and motivation more than simply calling someone you do not know just to inquire about their firm. For the most part, professional people love to hear from young students who are interested in what they do for a living. When you get the chance to talk with these professional business people about their careers, be sure to ask them about internships.

Another way of finding an internship or co-op is by searching the Internet on websites such as www.monster.com or www.headhunter.net. These two sites have great listings of all sorts of internships and co-ops available in your area.

One of the most notable internships I had the chance to participate in is one of the best for business students: Walt Disney World. To find out more about this internship, visit www.wdwcollegeprogram.com. There are endless opportunities for the young business entrepreneur at Walt Disney World. They accept all business majors and take applicants from around the world.

Success in the future is based on the effort and work you put into your education and work experience now. Do not wait until you are two months away from entering the workforce. Start right now to look for any opportunity you may find interesting. Today is not too soon to begin searching for your future.

Accounting

CHAPTER 2

AUDITOR

An auditor reviews financial statements, including the income statement, balance sheet, cash flow statement, and everything the company has completed to verify that everything they are reporting complies with generally accepted accounting principles (GAAP). Internal auditors work for the company they audit. External auditors are independent and are temporarily hired by a company to come in and make sure everything it is doing is correct. When the Internal Revenue Service calls you up and asks you to present your tax statements from the last three years, the tax auditor is the professional you consult.

The life of the auditor has changed dramatically from the boring and dull stereotype we have come to know. With all of the new accounting software currently available, most of the tedious work is now done on a computer. This allows the auditor to look more deeply into the companies they review.

Because of the amount of fraud taking place in the business world today (such as the accounting scandals

CAREER PROFILE
Entry salary range: $25,000 to $34,000 depending on education and credentials
Prerequisites: Bachelor's degree
Employers: Major corporations, accounting firms, and the government
Websites for Review: www.theiia.org (The Institute of Internal Auditors) www.isaca.org (Information Systems Audit and Control Association)

at Enron and WorldCom), the career of the auditor is rapidly becoming tainted. Laws and rules are becoming much more strict and the GAAP are meaning less and less to investors throughout the world who depend on the truth to determine whether or not they want to invest in a company.

An auditor is expected to read and understand financial statements thoroughly. Being able to verify this information by reviewing all of the actual entries within the ledger is crucial to the success of an auditor. While reviewing the company's numbers, they also review the effectiveness and efficiency of the company's procedures. The auditor will make suggestions on how the company may operate in a more timely manner, saving money and manpower.

With all of the functions of computers, business executives can make their decisions based on real-time data. A lot of data are immediately recorded, which allows upper and middle management to make more accurate decisions. This new luxury is simply another way to get more accurate data to the investors and improve the efficiency of securities markets.

Disadvantages

The life of an auditor can be stressful. There are so many rules and regulations to follow, including the GAAP, that things can easily be overlooked.

Some may consider the education required to become an accountant a disadvantage. To compete in our world today, most accountants obtain a bachelor's degree, a master's degree, and then sit for the four-part Certified Public Accountant (CPA) exam. Once you obtain your CPA, it is required that you complete a minimum of 120 hours of Continuing Professional Education (CPE) within a three-year-period to maintain your CPA certification.

Advantages

If you are an investigative type and enjoy looking back at previous records to ensure their credibility, this career may be for you. An auditor can be considered the police of the corporate world.

The stereotypical auditor who examines tax records is not the only kind of auditor. Auditors are found in all types of businesses. They check management procedures and ensure that they are effective and efficient. Within the brokerage industry, an auditor may be sent to ensure that the operations department as well as the brokers themselves are following all of the regulations of the Securities and Exchange Commission (SEC). If these regulations are not being followed, a much larger investigation may be ordered to determine what needs to be done to correct the problem.

Working as an auditor can be a rewarding career.

FINANCIAL MANAGER

If you have ever had the chance to read a financial statement, you can understand the complexity involved in its creation. The financial manager is responsible for ensuring these financial reports are correct and for tracking the cash flows from the company's liquid assets. To understand the importance of the financial manager, you must be able to understand the importance of liquidity within a business. If a business has no cash and all of its money is tied up in other projects, that company is in grave danger. It is crucial that a company keep a substantial amount of its cash on hand at all times for those unexpected times when liquidity is crucial.

CAREER PROFILE
Entry salary range: $35,000 to $45,000
Prerequisites: Bachelor's degree
Employers: All businesses, large and small
Websites for Review: www.fma.org (Financial Management Association International) www.nacm.org (National Association of Credit Management)

Generally, the career of a financial manager is not an entry-level position. It is a tough job and you must prove your analytical skills and abilities before you are promoted to this position. A financial manager can take the title of chief financial officer (CFO), treasurer, or vice president. All three of these positions are responsible for the flow of the company's cash. The chief financial officer has the most responsibilities and oversees all of the financial and accounting functions within a business. Generally, the CFO is the individual the other financial managers will report to with the data they have compiled concerning cash and cash equivalents.

There are three main financial reports the financial manager is responsible for: the income statement, balance sheet, and cash flow statement. These three documents are what analysts review when deciding whether to buy a certain stock or not. If these statements are correct and it looks as though the company is in a good financial situation, then investors will come and purchase stock within the company.

Also, when a company applies for credit with a bank, these three statements along with whatever documents the bank decides will be reviewed. The amount of the loan, interest rate of the loan, and the type of loan will all depend on these three statements.

Now that you know the importance of these financial statements, it is a bit clearer why the financial manager may be a bit overwhelmed within their career.

Disadvantages

If you are looking for a 40-hour-a-week job, this job is not for you. The responsibilities are extensive and it is the financial manager's job to make sure they are taken care of properly. Also, because of the extensive responsibility, the stress level may be high. When tax time comes around and all of the financial statements are due, it is your responsibility to review them to ensure the information is correct. Basically, you have the company in your hands. When you control the cash you control the business, so it is crucial you know exactly what strategy to implement.

Advantages

Financial managers are well respected. If you are in this position, you have worked hard to get there and will have a sense of accomplishment and a feeling of success. Also, when you are the one who controls the cash, you will also be the one making a great deal of cash. It is not uncommon for a financial manager, such as the CFO, to make well into six figures annually. Benefits such as a company car and company-sponsored vacations are also possibilities within this career.

If you are analytical and detail-oriented, a career as a financial manager just may be what you are looking for.

TAX ADVISOR

A tax advisor can come in a couple of different forms. The two most popular forms are in the advising of corporations and the advising of individuals. Both of these careers are in high demand. Consulting with individuals as to their options and how to minimize their taxes is a career to be considered. But in the next few pages we will be discussing the work of a corporate tax advisor. Because of recent fraud within large corporations, it is important to examine what exactly is expected of tax advisors, the corporations, and the individuals who make the decisions within the corporation.

CAREER PROFILE
Entry salary range: $34,000 to $42,000
Prerequisites: Bachelor's degree, CPA (Certified Public Accountant certification)
Employers: Computer manufacturers, banks, telecommunications companies, government, etc.
Websites for Review: www.acatcredentials.org (National Society of Accountants and the Accreditation Council for Accountancy and Taxation) www.imanet.org (Institute of Management Accountants)

A tax advisor is much more than just an individual who understands how to prepare a tax return properly. Although preparing taxes for the federal, state, and local levels is a major part of the job, it is not the most important task. A tax advisor researches and understands what the advantages and disadvantages are when acquiring a new business or divesting an old business. They understand why and when the best times are for investing in some financial assets such as other company's stocks, bonds, or other financial tools. They figure out how to minimize their company's taxes for the fiscal year. This can be done by forecasting future taxes with the use of models that represent the company's current position as well as using the company's past taxes to determine an approximation of this year's tax return.

Most companies operate with the intention to grow and get larger. They strategically purchase into new markets and sell out of old markets. The tax advisor will study models and run numbers to ensure that this decision is the best decision for the company's financial situation.

Disadvantages

The life of a tax advisor is demanding, especially when it comes to the end of a quarter or the end of a company's fiscal year. Many hours will be required of this individual and they will be expected to work weekends and holidays. During this time, it is crucial that the tax advisor ensure that all regulations set by the IRS and the SEC are followed correctly when reporting company earnings.

For the tax advisor, education never ends. Constantly learning the new tax laws implemented nearly every year is a major task. It is crucial that every law and rule be understood to ensure everything is done correctly. If things are done improperly, your company could be fined. Because of this, your company is responsible for providing continuing education courses and the proper tools to ensure it will benefit the most from the new tax laws.

Advantages

As a tax advisor you will have the opportunity to make a difference in your company's future. If you are good at what you do and understand what it means to minimize taxes, your job can be considered the most important within the company. The tax advisor can be the cause of a company reporting a loss or gain for its fiscal year. For example, Wall Street will always forecast the earnings for a company. If the company can beat this forecast, investors will want to reap the potential future profits earned from dividends and capital appreciation. If the tax advisor is well trained, he or she can find legal and ethical methods to help the company beat Wall Street's estimates.

Working as a tax advisor will provide you with a nice life. This career is demanding but when tax season has passed, the life of the tax advisor relaxes as well. This career is never boring and new adventures arise monthly. When a company is in the process or thinking of entering a new business merger or buy-out, you will be the first to know because it is you who will research the positive and negative effects of this purchase. This career has nothing typical about it and keeps you on your toes. If you enjoy constantly incurring new tasks, the tax advising career may be for you.

BUDGET ANALYST

If you ever have the chance to work for a relatively large company, you will be given a budget for the department you control. The department you are working in is responsible for remaining under that budget. A lot of times, the department manager's bonus may depend on how well they stay under their budget. Simply put, a budget is an allowance for any certain department and they should not spend more than that limit. There are situations when the unexpected comes up and either you or a member of the board will have to approve an allowance for this situation.

CAREER PROFILE
Entry salary range: $23,000 to $27,000
Prerequisites: Bachelor's degree
Employers: Financial institutions, retail stores, hospitals, public schools, and colleges
Websites for Review: www.nasbo.org (National Association of State Budget Officers) www.agacgfm.org (Advancing Government Accountability)

As the president of the Economics and Finance Club in college, I had the opportunity to head the Budget Committee where I prepared a budget for an entire festival of games, rides, and foods. Although a festival is not a corporation, it is still a profit-seeking event with many different committees that acquire costs that must be monitored to maximize the profits of the entire event. Each committee working at the festival was required to prepare a proposal for my review. I then reviewed each of the proposals and decided what they did not need, what they could do less expensively than their projected budget, and what was close to being the actual cost.

The next step was to figure out just how I was going to distribute the limited resources equally but effectively and efficiently. As with all corporations, the financial resources for the festival were extremely limited. There was only so much money I was able to give to each committee of the festival. The distribution of the money throughout all departments was the toughest part of preparing the budget, and it is the same experience you will get within a corporation. Every department within the corporation feels like it needs more money than what you have allowed it . This is almost always true! If you were to grant every department all the money they wanted, there would be no reason to prepare a budget. Distributing resources to departments causes each department manager to allocate resources to maximize the total output. This may be experienced by cutting hours, purchasing cheaper office machines, minimizing the use of paper, or even temporarily or permanently laying off some of the employees within the department.

Disadvantages
Each department will at some time give you a hard time about your decisions. A department will request $10,000 dollars from you, but you believe it can maximize output with only $7,000. Now the department manager is upset because his or her job just got a lot tougher. Either the manager will make his or her department run on the $7,000 or will prepare a proposal and come back to you for more money. You must stand

firm, unless the proposal is persuasive and your calculations were incorrect.

Each year a new budget is prepared for the entire firm. During this time of the year, the budget analyst will be expected to work more than 40 hours a week including some weekends if the work needs to be done. There will also be strict deadlines and long hours.

Advantages

If you want to know how it feels to have power within a company, just be in control of the money supply. Every department manager will bring you gifts on Christmas, wish you a happy birthday, and offer to wash your car on the weekend. (Well, perhaps that is a slight exaggeration.).

As a budget analyst, it is your duty to distribute an efficient amount of monetary resources to the other departments to allow them to do their jobs efficiently and effectively. For example, if the advertising department needs $4,000 for a new computer system and you feel that a cheaper computer system can do the same job, it is your responsibility to ensure that the cheaper computer system is bought unless there is an excellent reason why the more expensive system is needed. If the $4,000 computer must be purchased, you may be required to take the extra money from another department, causing yourself headaches from the other department.

STAFF ACCOUNTANT

If you have a four-year degree in accounting and are looking to get your feet wet in the accounting field before you decide to sit for the CPA, staff accountant is an excellent place to begin. The staff accountant generally requires no experience, just a typical four-year degree in accounting. Staff accountants are employed virtually everywhere and deal with a lot of the book-entry positions. Many accountants specialize in taxes, financial planning, cost analyzing, auditing, and so forth. A staff accountant is not yet specialized but will gain the experience to make a decision as to specialty.

CAREER PROFILE
Entry salary range: $20,000 to $24,000
Prerequisites: Bachelor's degree
Employers: Telecommunications, government, entertainment, universities, etc.
Websites for Review: www.aicpa.org (American Institute of Certified Public Accountants) www.imanet.org (Institute of Management Accountants)

Staff accountants must be analytical. They are expected to ensure that accounting principles are followed when preparing reports for analysis. They must also have the knowledge to set up ledgers and journals and be able to keep track of receivables and payables to maintain an accurate record of the company's books.

Proficiency with computers is a must since most of your daily functions will involve the use of a computer. Since the staff accountant deals with the company's daily procedures, a constant evolution of procedures will take place to continue making the accounting system more effective as well as more efficient.

As in every career, good oral and written communication skills are a must for the staff accountant. The information relayed between different people within each organization is so crucial that if the information is incorrect, the company can face heavy fines. At all times you must expect an auditor to walk in the front door so your work can be audited. As the auditor reviews your work, he or she will be critiquing you and ensuring that your organizational and communication skills are appropriate for your position.

Disadvantages

Staff accountant is an entry-level position that can be tedious. Tracking all entries for an entire year can be exhausting. Also, the staff accountant has the duty of dealing with anyone in the company who is seeking accounting advice. It is your job to handle all of these questions and requests in a timely manner.

As with any career in accounting, the rules and regulations change on a yearly basis. This can cause your job to be stressful if you do not maintain the knowledge it takes to do the job. Your firm will be expected to provide you with the tools necessary to keep your knowledge of the law up to speed.

Advantages

This is an excellent way to make your way through the field of accounting. The staff accountant is an entry-level position, so where you go from there is your choice. You will gain experience in nearly every field and get a feeling for the accounting principles and procedures for that company.

When you work as an accountant, you will have a feeling of accomplishment at the end of the fiscal year.

Networking

The most effective way to ensure a job right after graduation is through the use of networking with individuals associated with potential employers. Networking gives you an opportunity to meet people, gain experience, and show potential employers you are serious about gaining experience for the long-term outcome of your career. Not only does this allow you the chance to meet with people who may be potential employers, but it also enables you to make sure you are getting into a career that fits your personality.

How does a student begin networking? This really is not as hard as it may seem. If you have found a career that may be of some interest, contacting someone in that career is the first step. In my experience, just about everyone is willing to sit down with you for 15 to 20 minutes and talk about what they do on a daily basis, so do not be afraid to ask. Let them know you are serious about your future and you may want to be in their shoes in the future but are not certain just yet.

If they accept, and they most likely will, act and dress professionally, and portray confidence but do not overdue it. When you go into their office, be friendly, greet them with a handshake, make eye contact, and ask all the questions you can in the amount of time you have. Do not walk into their office unprepared.

Do not limit yourself to one person. Think of careers that may interest you and network with people in those fields. Talk to a couple of people at the same place and ask for their advice. Remember, these people were once in your shoes. They know what it takes and how to get where they are now, so do not be shy.

Networking is the most powerful tool you can use for achieving the job you want right out of college. As most people will tell you, it is not just what you know but who you know that helps you get ahead in the world. Having contacts around your hometown is ideal for the short-term and long-term success of your future.

Finance and Economics

CHAPTER 3

FINANCIAL ADVISOR

One of the toughest jobs in the business world is financial advisor. To be a financial advisor, the ability to analyze stocks, read reports, and manage an individual's money is only part of being successful. The most crucial part of success is being able to form and mold relationships with different individuals and maintain these relationships throughout the client's life. An intelligent investor who understands the market and risk, can still make a poor financial advisor; but a bad investor who is new to the market may still have a shot at being a successful financial advisor.

Integrity is crucial to every job. As a financial advisor, this is not only true, but critical to the overall success of the individual. A client must believe the financial advisor is not only knowledgeable about the subject, but will do everything in his or her power to make sure the investor's money is as safe as possible.

Thanks to technology, the technical abilities of the advisor are far less than they were 20 years ago. Most

CAREER PROFILE
Entry salary range: $23,000 to $30,000, or a commission-based salary
Prerequisites: Bachelor's degree, series 7 and 66
Employers: Companies providing financial services for customers seeking advice
Websites for Review: www.cfp-board.org (Certified Financial Planner Board of Standards) www.sia.com (Securities Industry Association) www.ml.com (Merrill Lynch)

financial advisors do not analyze charts, financial statements, cash flow statements, or annual reports produced by the company. Today, most brokers are more responsible for knowing what tools to use and why they should use them. Most investment firms have stock analysts in their head office who are responsible for studying certain companies and deciding whether a stock, bond, or mutual fund is a good investment or not. It is up to the advisor to read the analyst's reports and then decide on the risk factor for the individual client.

A good financial advisor working hard for his or her clients can maintain an above-average lifestyle while making friends in all walks of life. Reading the analyst's reports and maintaining the integrity needed for this career are two of the most important ingredients of being a financial advisor.

Although a college education should be considered the bare minimum, it is only the beginning of your learning experience. There are two examinations that must be passed before you can begin prospecting your future clients. The first examination is a two-part test that lasts about three hours per part. This examination is the series 7 and will cover most of the financial tools you will use as a financial advisor including equities, debentures, mutual funds, options, and so forth.

The series 66 is a combination of the series 63 and 65. These cover the laws and rules of being a financial advisor. These two examinations are the two most important examinations but are by far not the only two examinations. Also, as a financial advisor, there are several examinations, such as the General Principal License, also known as the series 24, you can take to give credibility to yourself and your business.

Disadvantages

Right out of college, it is difficult for an individual to succeed in the marketplace. There is a lot of competition in the United States with discount brokers and online brokers. The target market for an inexperienced financial advisor are individuals with an approximate net worth of $50,000 to $100,000. This amount of money is ideal for a new advisor to get his or her feet wet. Unfortunately, clients with $50,000 tend to use discount brokers or online trading because the commissions are so much cheaper. A financial advisor will charge approximately $50 for every trade when the exact same trade can be done online for $14.99 to $19.99 per trade.

Generally, this career is 100 percent commission-based. For an individual with a spouse and a couple of kids, there is a lot of risk. A young person such as yourself, with no dependents, should consider that the potential returns may far outweigh the risk of fluctuating commission-based income.

Advantages

When a financial advisor is able to penetrate the market and create his or her own client base, the incentives are endless. Once the first few years are over, and you are well on your way to being a successful financial advisor, you are in charge of your own business. You determine the hours you will work, the days you take off, and how much money you are going to make. The greatest advantage is that it is almost the same as opening your own business, only you do not have to put any money up front and if you fail, you do not lose thousands of dollars.

Today, more and more financial advisors are moving toward fee-based accounts. These are accounts that earn the broker money annually whether or not the client is trading. This is ideal for the financial advisor and is yet another advantage for the broker because it adds some security to his or her income.

TRUST OFFICER

A trust officer can take many shapes and forms. The most popular is that of the personal trust officer, which is similar to a financial advisor. Trust officers manage billions of dollars in all sorts of assets. A personal trust is a financial tool that allows the correct distribution of the client's assets upon his or her death. These assets can consist of real estate, stocks, mutual funds, money, and valuables such as jewelry, artwork, real estate, and any other item that is of value to the client.

CAREER PROFILE
Entry salary range: $23,000 to $30,000
Prerequisites: Bachelor's degree
Employers: All major banks and financial institutions that offer trusts as a financial tool
Websites for Review: www.aba.com (American Bankers Association) www.afpoline.org (Association for Financial Professionals)

A trust officer uses living trusts, IRAs, and a number of other planning tools to ensure estate plans are carried out as the person wishes once he or she has passed away. The trust officer must be knowledgeable of the tools to shelter or minimize tax liabilities, such as estate and probate taxes.

A trust officer must be trusted by his or her clients. A lot of what a trust officer does happens after a client's death, although they do a lot while the client is alive as well. Your clients should feel secure that their estate plans will be carried through, so it is your job to make them feel good about making you their trust officer.

Individuals may want their estate to be distributed between their heirs, charities, or several other designations set prior to their death. A good example of why a trust officer is needed would be for those couples who have children who are not capable of taking care of themselves. What happens to these children when their parents pass away? Who is going to take care of them? The parents can set up a trust to pay for the care that is necessary for the child's well-being. This is just one more of many options an individual has when using a trust.

Disadvantages

One major disadvantage most trust officers will face is dealing with the children of the deceased. When the children's parents die, they think that all assets are handed over to them immediately. When a trust is created, the parents of the children may set up a payment schedule that must be followed. There are some individuals who do not know how to handle their own finances. When given money, they want to spend it immediately and get themselves into trouble. With this payment schedule, the beneficiaries get an allowance and nothing more. This allowance is given to them until the trust runs out of assets. This sometimes results in lawsuits, which can make the trust officer's life stressful.

Also, another disadvantage in this career is that there are many misunderstandings in this area, making the trust officer's job difficult.

Advantages

There is no better opportunity to help an individual control, distribute, and maintain wealth than the use of a personal trust. It is the trust officer who will search for different ways to help individuals minimize risk and taxes and maintain the assets they have worked a lifetime to obtain. People have different needs so different tools must be used to help them.

Many older people are scared about what will happen with their assets once they die. These individuals want certain things to happen with their assets but know that a will does not always stand up in court. Individuals who have split families that want to do different things with the assets are likely to fight a will in court. A trust, on the other hand, will stand up in court and your assets will be distributed just as you wish. Having this power as a trust officer is rewarding. If having the need to help people in your life is important to you and you enjoy working with finances, a career as a trust officer might be ideal.

BROKERAGE OPERATIONS SPECIALIST

If you enjoy working with the stock market but do not want to be a salesperson or sell stocks yourself, this could be an excellent career for you. A brokerage operations specialist works behind the scenes ensuring that everything is taken care of properly. If the broker is having a problem or has made a mistake, it is usually up to the brokerage operations specialist to fix the problem. Although individuals who invest with the company do not see the operations specialist, the company could not function without them.

CAREER PROFILE
Entry salary range: $23,000 to $27,000
Prerequisites: Bachelor's degree
Employers: Banks and brokerage firms hire about 95 percent of all brokerage operations specialists
Websites for Review: www.nasdr.com (National Association of Securities Dealers) www.sia.com (Securities Industry Association)

The brokerage operations specialist is responsible for nearly everything but the actual selling of any financial tools. They are responsible for the opening of new accounts, depositing and issuing checks, depositing and issuing stock certificates, verifying orders, transferring accounts in and out, IRA distributions, account maintenance, and sorting out any problems the brokers or the clients may have.

In this line of business, it is impossible to list everything that is done because every day, something new happens. The broker is sometimes completely dependent on you. When they are out of the office, on vacation, or cannot be found and their clients want to make trades, they will call you. It is up to you to take their order and process it immediately. Generally, you will not give advice to the clients but simply take the order. Also, when the client is upset about something, the broker will generally call you to fix the problem with the account, statements, or any errors they may find.

Disadvantages

When you deal with the stock market, you are under a highly regulated system. It is your responsibility to ensure that your firm is following National Association of Securities Dealers (NASD) regulations or you could find yourself in trouble with the law. In today's world, money laundering, insider trading, and any other fraud is watched closely. These criminal acts are punishable with jail terms and high monetary penalties.

When you have 20 or so brokers to take care of, all of your work can clutter your mind. These brokers expect for you to put them first to ensure their clients' well-being. It is up to you to prioritize and ensure the most important things are taken care of first. You will find yourself under a lot of deadlines at the same time throughout the day. All of these deadlines must be met or you could find yourself out of compliance with NASD regulations.

When problems come up, it is usually your problem. Usually the broker has little or no authority to make changes in their clients' accounts, commissions, or in any other area of business. It is their job to sell and your job to make sure everything is in order.

Advantages

If experience in this field is what you are looking for, you are in luck. There is no other career right after college that will lead you into a financial career with experience in the brokerage industry than working in the operations department. Within the operations department all of the laws, rules and regulations of the brokerage industry can be learned. You can almost think of this career as a continuing education for your bachelor's degree. This is because you will learn every part of the business, except for selling. You will see how people handle their clients and learn what to do and what not to do. Most firms will sponsor your brokerage licenses such as the series 7, which is the most important license to obtain, the series 66, and your life and health insurance licenses. Acquiring these licenses will open a lot of doors.

As an operations specialist you will learn most of the important skills you will need to become a financial planner, trust officer, or any other financial planning opportunity. You will learn the dos and don'ts of the business. Making good use of the education allowances your firm allows will ensure for a better and brighter future in the brokerage industry.

CREDIT ANALYST

A credit analyst's main focus is whether or not to loan money to individual consumers or major corporations. They use financial statements, such as the income statement, the balance sheet, and the cash flow statement to determine if an individual or a business is qualified for the loan. Sometimes, the analyst will go back as far as three years reviewing past financial statements to make sure that this company is on their way to becoming profitable. Many companies will find themselves working for years and going nowhere and it is up to the credit analyst to notice these trends and put a stop to them. For the most part, we will be discussing the career of a credit analyst who reviews the credit of a corporation or local business. Basically, working with numbers and analyzing financial data is most of what a credit analyst does throughout their day.

CAREER PROFILE
Entry salary range: $25,000 to $29,000
Prerequisites: Bachelor's degree
Employers: Banks, savings banks, and other financial institutions that offer loans to consumers and businesses
Websites for Review: www.teleport.com/ric (Credit Management and Information Support) www.nacm.org (National Association of Credit)

When lending money to a company, cash is what makes the difference. If a company has little cash, no one wants to lend it money. Lending money on expected earnings, which is what happened with a lot of the dot-com businesses, is a bad way of lending large sums of money. A credit analyst must use financial ratios and computer software to build models to better understand their financial conditions. The financial statements are carefully reviewed and checked for liquidity, current short-term and long-term debts, and other liabilities that could cause the company to default on the loan.

Companies also carry a credit rating just like individuals. Some companies have such a good credit rating a credit analyst does not really have to determine whether or not they should get the loan. On the other side, a start-up company that wants to run a business off of the Internet will find it difficult to get a loan from the local bank at a reasonable interest rate.

Companies may need more money to build, venture into new markets, or increase their debt. Why would a company want to increase their debt? Some companies who seem to be good potential companies for buyouts or acquisitions will increase their total debt so other companies will not want to purchase them anymore. This is simply a strategy to maintain a young company that wants to continue to grow on their own.

Disadvantages

Reviewing all of these statements can be quite boring. If you are an individual who does not want to review credit in a cubicle while running numbers and ratios through your head, this career is not for you. This individual must be prepared to evaluate the risks of lending a company the money they need to become more profitable and then present their suggestions to the bank executives. These suggestions should include everything that is found in the financial reports, a brief history of the company, and their recommendation of how much the business should be allowed to borrow.

Generally, the credit analyst position is somewhat of a dead end but will provide you with the right experience to move on in other areas within the banking industry.

Advantages

The career of a credit analyst is one of the best lead-in jobs a college graduate could find in the business. It is an excellent opportunity to meet contacts at local businesses. It is also one of the best careers to have when trying to break into the banking business. Dealing with money, financial statements, and credit will provide you with the proper experience to make it to the top if you are willing to put forth the effort it will take to get you there.

Generally, the credit analyst reviews credit for major loans. They are usually one of the first to know about large projects within their city. Again, this allows you to meet city officials and important business owners within the local area, bettering your chances for success in the future. Once again, it's not always what you know, but who you know!

LOAN APPROVER

Millions of loans are approved every day throughout the United States. These loans can be used for purchasing furniture, cars, swimming pools or even houses. It is the loan approver's job to look at the consumer's financial situation and credit history and then make a decision based on their feelings about their overall character.

The loan approver's job is tough. Not only do they have to make a decision as whether to give them a loan or not, but they also have to decide what kind of loan to give them. Some individuals qualify for an unsecured loan with no collateral backing the loan, others must secure the loan with the deed to their house, title to their car, or something else of value so that if the consumer defaults on the loan, the loan approver can come pick up the collateral to pay for the loan.

CAREER PROFILE
Entry salary range: $19,000 to $25,000
Prerequisites: Bachelor's degree
Employers: Banks, savings banks, and financial institutions that offer personal loans or loans through retailers
Websites for Review: www.mbaa.org (Mortgage Bankers Association of America) www.aba.com (American Bankers Association)

It is the responsibility of the loan approver to lend money only to those people capable of repaying the loans. A loan approver will pull an individual's credit history from one of the three main credit agencies: Trans

Union, Experian, or Equifax. After pulling the credit history, the next step is to ensure that the individual's income is sufficient to cover all of his or her current bills. If this amount is sufficient, the individual's repayment history will be examined.

In my experience as a retail credit analyst, there were individuals who would earn well over $100,000 a year but would be turned down because they did not pay their bills. People with poor credit may have to pay for everything in cash, or if they do get a loan, they may have to pay a higher interest rate because they are considered a higher risk.

If the consumer does meet the requirements for the loan, the loan approver must decide what kind of loan the individual requires. If the individual has a spotless credit history, they may get an unsecured loan. This is usually a revolving credit, similar to a credit card but without the card. A revolving credit account will allow the person to continue to borrow a certain amount without reapplying every time. If the individual has a good credit rating, but the loan approver still has doubts, he or she may decide to require that collateral be put down in support of the loan. This reduces the company's risk of default. If the consumer does default, whatever was used as collateral may be repossessed to cover the expense of the loan.

Disadvantages

At times, the stress level of the loan approver may be quite high. When you are forced to turn down an individual for a loan they really need, you may find yourself being yelled at or even threatened. These types of situations happen rarely but throughout your career, this situation may arise. Also, as I have witnessed, turning down a family that is down on their luck is also a difficult situation. But sometimes it is impossible to find ways to help such people. This can be emotionally upsetting.

Advantages

While turning down a loan to individuals who really need the money but cannot qualify can be upsetting, approving a loan for a young couple about to buy their first home is satisfying. This type of reward come quite often.

This profession is one of the largest professions in finance. Every financial institution in the loan business employs loan approvers. The financial services industry is growing rapidly and this profession is one of the first few steps to progressing within a bank or other institution. If you enjoy working with people and numbers, this career could be ideal for you.

INSURANCE AGENT

An insurance agent works for one or more insurance companies selling their products to individuals who want to pass their risk on to someone else. It is the insurance company's job to take the premiums from many to support the losses of a few. When working as an insurance agent, one may find it an excellent way to make a comfortable living. The job is tough and keeps you busy for your entire life, but it becomes a part of you. As an insurance agent, you are able to get involved in people's lives and when they are in need of some help, you are there to help them. Sometimes, insurance agents are considered heroes to many people.

CAREER PROFILE
Entry salary range: Commission-based
Prerequisites: Bachelor's degree
Employers: Independent insurance sales facilities or financial institutions that provide insurance as a means of financial planning
Websites for Review: www.independentagent.com (Independent Insurance Agents of America) www.pianet.com (National Association of Professional Insurance Agents)

Just as in any sales profession, insurance agents must commit to their clients. You must possess the ability to persuade these individuals that you are the right insurance agent for them. This includes having confidence, enthusiasm, and a good work ethic. As an insurance agent in your beginning years, you will spend many hours trying to build your client base. It is up to you to find these individuals through friends, family, cold calling, and simply meeting new people every day. When meeting with these people, it is crucial you are sincere about your career and the individuals you are trying to help. An individual can feel whether you are sincere or just giving them a line that you repeat on a daily basis. In today's world, an insurance agent is not just a salesperson, but also a risk manager.

The most important part of this career is that your clients are your main priority. These clients are your business and without them, there is no business or income for you.

Disadvantages

As the insurance agent, it is in your best interest to ensure that your clients understand and accept the contract you are trying to sell them. Say, for instance, you sell auto insurance to a client. This individual is now insured by the company you sponsor. The next day, this individual gets into an auto accident that was his or her fault. It is later determined the wreck occurred because the client was drag racing. The following day, this particular individual pays you a visit to file a claim. You must point out a clause in the contract indicating that the insurance agent is not responsible for the damages because the client was drag racing, something considered to be against the law.

Another disadvantage to the career of insurance agent is the rejection involved. When you begin your career, cold calling, knocking on doors, and meeting new people every day are a must to survive. It is said that of 10 new prospects you talk to, there will only be one sale. Some people may find themselves so discouraged by time they get to the ninth person they just want to quit.

The last major disadvantage to this career are the long hours that you must be willing to put in to be successful. You may be required to work 55 to 65 hours a week at times. Basically, you are a true entrepreneur and it is your responsibility to either survive or fail.

Advantages

Although an insurance agent may be seen as a bad guy sometimes, it is always the insurance agent who gets the call from a client who is in trouble. In this situation, it is time for the hero to come out in the insurance agent. Imagine a family's house burning down and they lost everything. If that family has the proper insurance, the agent will then provide them with the money they need to make them whole again. There is nothing scarier than losing everything you have in a fire. Some items in the house are irreplaceable because of their sentimental value, but most possessions can be replaced. It is these situations that allow the insurance agent to save the day for families. The career of an insurance agent is a fine business where you have the chance to do good things for people.

ACTUARY

Since there is no chapter for mathematics in this book, I have put it in the finance and economics chapter. The role of the actuary is so crucial to the insurance world and so in demand throughout the nation that any student who has a strong background in mathematics and business should consider this as a future career. As in most careers, good communication skills are crucial to your success. After your research and analysis, you will be asked to present your determinations in front of the decision makers for the company.

CAREER PROFILE
Entry salary range: $30,000 to $35,000
Prerequisites: Bachelor's degree in mathematics, statistics, or actuarial science
Employers: The government and insurance companies
Websites for Review: www.soa.org (Society of Actuaries)   www.casact.org (Casualty Actuarial Society)   www.aspa.org (American Society of Pension Actuaries)

Approximately 75 percent of all actuaries are employed by the government or insurance companies. The actuary studies statistics, probabilities, and mathematic models to determine the premium that consumers are paying for insurance. The fact that insurance is commonly higher for males than it is for females was determined by an actuary who saw the statistics and determined that males are more likely to have accidents. Those who have speeding tickets and accidents or who have been convicted of driving under the influence of alcohol also pay a higher premium than safer drivers because of the findings of an actuary.

For the actuary, there are a series of 10 examinations that must be completed to be considered a Fellow. The title of Fellow is what most employers expect from actuaries they hire. The process of becoming a Fellow can take up to 10 years to complete. The Society of Actuaries and the Casualty Actuarial Society are the only two organizations that administer the 10 examinations to become a Fellow. With each examination that is passed, your income can be expected to increase. But until the first examination is passed, the chance of finding a job is nearly impossible. The first test is only offered every six months so it is crucial to take the test as soon as possible.

Disadvantages

Depending on your personality, the life of an actuary may be rather dull. They spend most of their time behind a desk, playing with facts and figures to determine the outcome of certain events in order to examine the risks of possible accidents. These days usually consist of normal eight-to-five workdays.

Also, the 10 tests are nothing short of an extreme and intense expedition. The first test has a 30 percent pass/fail rate.

Advantages

The life of an actuary can be rewarding. This job requires a lot of accomplishment and puts you behind the wheel of the company. It is up to you to determine the rates of the insurance premiums. The more accurate you are in your facts and figures, the more profitable the company will be. The rates must be competitive yet still provide your company with sufficient earning.

Actuaries are considered to have an extremely stress-free career with a rewarding paycheck. Working for an insurance company in an office running numbers is generally stress-free except for the rare occasion when you may find yourself facing a major deadline. Actuaries are also in such high demand that entering the field and advancing is becoming easier and easier. In the next few years the expected growth will be so great that entering right after college with an above-average salary is highly possible as long as the first of the 10 examinations has been passed.

Resume Building

The biggest misconception about a resume is that it is created to get you a job. In fact, the resume is simply used to earn you the possibility of receiving an interview.

To begin, gather all of the information of your professional career and education. Since you are just beginning in your career search, it is important to emphasize your education qualifications since your work experience is probably limited. When outlining your education, include everything you have done. All of your extracurricular activities should be listed as well as the position that you held while belonging to organizations. This provides you with the chance to display your energies outside of the classroom.

Key words are important as well. Many large corporations will place your resume in a scanner looking for a couple of key words. If these words are not found, your resume will be automatically shredded. This is simply to help them minimize the amount of time and energy that must be put into reviewing the thousands of resumes they receive each year. Some key words consist of: teamed, partnered, team work, committee, and other words that prove that you are capable of working with other people in a team effort and fitting in with their work environment. Carefully selecting the words you choose is not only good for your resume but will benefit you throughout your professional career.

It is recommended you have a professional review your resume. With little experience at this stage of your life, it is difficult to determine exactly what the next person may be looking for in a candidate for their job position. Allow either someone in a human resources department or a guidance counselor to review your resume and give you some constructive criticism about how to make it stronger and more appealing. In my own experience, every individual you show your resume to will tell you something different. It is important to pick a style you like and feel represents you and your professional abilities. This resume is a tool you will use throughout your whole life. It's a short story about your capabilities, life, and achievements.

On the next few pages you will find a couple of examples of good resumes. These resumes have already been reviewed by several individuals in a human resources department.

Jennifer J. Jones
1336 Lily Valley
Evans, OH 20181
(020)429-8666
jj@evans.dom

Objective:
To work in a position that utilizes my relationship skills and technical abilities and where I can continue to grow professionally.

Education:
Evans College   Evans, OH   May 2003 Graduate
- GPA (3.2/4.0)
- Bachelor of Science Degree Candidate majoring in Finance and minoring in Economics

Internships:
Evans Financial   Evans, OH   May 2001–November 2002
- Researched stocks and mutual funds using Morning Star, S&P, and Merrill Lynch Reports
- Assisted in the prospecting of current and future clients by cold calling
- Assist in the general organization of daily activities and in the presentation of client proposals

Work Experience:
Brokerage Assistant
E & G, Inc.   Evans, OH   December 2002–Present
- Preparing proposals and presentations with MS PowerPoint, Excel, Word, and various other software
- Teaming with the vice president and the assistant vice president to increase daily production
- Contacting clients to organize appointments
- Simplifying complicated fact sheets for the clients' benefit using Microsoft Excel
- Analyzing clients' accounts to reduce fees in accounts prior to the selling of securities

Jennifer J. Jones, page 2

Clubs and Organizations:

Institute of Management Accountants	Associate Director
Omicron Delta Epsilon	International Honor Society in Economics
Alpha Kappa Psi	The Professional Business Fraternity
Finance Club	President/Treasurer
Speaking Eagles (Toast Masters)	Secretary
Investment Club	President/Co-founder
Rotary Club	Mentor Program
Accounting Club	Active Member

Computer Skills:

Knowledgeable with troubleshooting a Windows-based computer.
Also, knowledgeable of Microsoft Office including Microsoft Word,
Excel, Access, and Power Point

Michael Andrew Frost
10761 Wex Court
Hill, CA 72238
(001)938-2420
maf@hill.dom

Objective: To obtain a position as a Marketing Specialist.

Professional Profile:
Bachelor of Science in Marketing
Two Years of Marketing Experience
Effective Planning and Organizational Skills
Ability to Work Well Both Independently and in a Team Environment
Excellent Interpersonal/Communications Skills
Ability to Successfully Manage Multiple Priorities and Assignments.
Analytical Skills

Education:
Hill University   Hill, CA
Bachelor of Science in Marketing   December 2003
Graduate
Cumulative GPA 3.6/4.0

Relevant Work Experience:
Assistant Credit Specialist
Teacher's Credit Union   Hill, CA August 2003 - Present
Develop and Maintain Long-Term Business Relationships
Originate and Process Mortgage Loans
Create Prospecting and Advertisement Material
Establish and Evaluate Needs-Based Retirement Plans for Clients
Provide Health and Life Insurance
Establish Budget Plans for Clients

Honors and Activities:
Deans List
Honors List
Marketing Club
Alpha Kappa Psi

Management

CHAPTER 4

MANAGER

Management exists within every form of business. Within each of these fields is first-line management, middle management, or upper management for nearly every department within the company. Education and/or experience determine the level of management. Here, we will concentrate on the first-line manager because that is where most individuals with a management degree right out of college will begin. Rarely will a graduate with little or no experience go right into middle or upper management.

CAREER PROFILE
Entry salary range: $22,000 to $28,000
Prerequisites: Associate degree
Employers: All areas of employment
Websites for Review: www.nma1.org (National Management Association) www.amanet.org (American Management Association)

The main goal of the first-line manager is to ensure that the plans of upper and middle management are carried out. Most first-line managers will work with the employees and must learn to instruct them efficiently and effectively. The first-line manager must recognize the strong and weak spots of their employees and place them where each employee can maximize his or her potential talents and benefit the firm the most.

Making schedules can be a hassle when every individual employee is unique. Some people need certain days off and others need to work only in the morning. When you supervise 45 employees and have to make the schedule for each one of them, your job can become somewhat difficult at times.

The hiring and firing process is also a task that may become second nature to the first-line manager. Since the first-line manager works side-by-side with most of the employees, it is up to them to make sure the employees are capable of handling their jobs. If employees are not capable of handling what is expected of them, it is up to the supervisor to take them off the payroll list permanently.

Disadvantages

First-line managers who deal with high turnover ratios find their job to be stressful. It is tough to take the plans of upper and middle management and make employees work when they sometimes have little or no dedication to the employer. You must also figure out how to motivate employees. First-line management for the most part does not consist of a regular set schedule. Evenings, weekends, and holidays may be required.

When working with the public, the first-line management usually hears all complaints. Complaints come in a lot more frequently than praise so each complaint needs to be handled differently from the rest. It is crucial that you, as the supervisor, treat each problem as if it is top priority to ensure the customer's complete satisfaction.

Advantages

Having a career as a first-line manager may cause some stress in your life, but you are in control of your future. Although sometimes you have to play the bad guy, there are many opportunities to play the good guy as well. When employees need help, they depend on you to take care of their problems. When things go wrong, you will hear the wrath of customers as well as your boss, but when things go well, you will hear praise and perhaps receive a bonus.

When working as a first-line manager, you have plenty of opportunity to grow within the company. Once this career has been tackled and you have proven yourself, it will be time for your promotion. When you make it to middle management, you then begin learning the planning process. Working at the head of a department and ensuring that the first-line managers are doing what they need to be doing can be rewarding in itself. In this position, you will gain enough knowledge of the business to understand what it was for the last several years your bosses were trying to get you to do. Middle and upper management look at the bigger picture. They focus more on company goals whereas the first-line manager tends to focus on departmental goals.

Many people will find life as a first-line manager rewarding in the short run as well as the long run. Being able to set goals for your employees as well as yourself can be rewarding when all goals are met.

HUMAN RESOURCES MANAGER

Almost everyone who is reading this book has probably applied for a job at some time or another. Although you may have applied within a business that does not have a human resources department, it is still up to someone in the company to play the role of human resources manager.

The primary role of the human resources manager is the job selection process. Some jobs require such a unique and special individual that the search can go on for days, weeks, or even months. As a human resources manager with a local bank, filling a job might not be too difficult depending on what the position is, but imagine what it is like for a multi-million dollar company. They receive thousands of applications every year for positions within one of their departments. In fact, they receive so many applications and resumes, they screen them with a machine that scans for qualifying words. If they are not found, the resume or application is discarded immediately, without ever being read.

CAREER PROFILE
Entry salary range: $22,000 to $29,000
Prerequisites: Bachelor's degree
Employers: Colleges, banks, the government, hospitals, travel agencies, etc.
Websites for Review: www.pihra.org (Professionals in Human Resources Association) www.shrm.org (Society for Human Resource Management)

Working in a human resources department will keep you busy. The human resources department caters to other departments in the company reviewing applications that come in, interviewing potential employees, dealing with conflicts between individuals within the firm, and terminating employees.

Selecting the right person for the job is more than just a challenge for a company. If the wrong person is selected for the wrong job, the money spent on processing the paperwork, training the new employee, and all the other expenses is wasted. Being critical of each applicant is crucial and can be tedious.

Although the hiring process for the company may be the largest part of the human resources manager's day, it is not all they are responsible for. When conflicts arise within a company such as sexual harassment, verbal harassment, or fighting, it is the HR manager's job to resolve these conflicts. The human resources department is responsible for ensuring that every employee has a safe and sound place to work.

Disadvantages

Working as a human resources manager has a few unique disadvantages. If you are soft-hearted and not capable of terminating an employee, this career may not be for you. When a termination must take place, crying can be hard to see or deal with. When an individual has a family to feed it can be difficult.

At times it can even be dangerous. Yelling can take place, fights can break out, and threats are sometimes experienced. Although this is not typical, it is still a possibility to consider before taking on this career.

Advantages

Probably the most rewarding part of the job is when you have the opportunity to call an individual and offer him or her a job. When you hear their excitement, you too have a good feeling inside of you. It is like sending a kid to Walt Disney World for the first time. You are the hero, even if just for a minute.

Also, if an employee is having trouble in his or her position, either with an internal or external conflict, and is not sure how to handle it, he or she may come to you. If it is a problem you can solve, you can be the one to help them out. If you are unable to intercede for them, you can give advice, show how the problem might be solved, and at least lighten the stress. If you enjoy working with people and helping them on a daily basis, this job could be your future career.

PURCHASING MANAGER

The next time you walk into a retail store, look around at everything in the store. Each item was purchased by a purchasing manager. It is the purchasing manager's job to decide what is a good purchase. Basically, they purchase the highest quality products at the lowest possible prices. A purchasing manager's job has really been made a lot easier since the implementation of computers because now, when an item is scanned by a cashier, the computer makes a record of that sale and that item is then listed on the purchase list for the next purchase date. Sometimes, it is even made easier. When the product is scanned, the warehouse is notified immediately for the next delivery.

CAREER PROFILE
Entry salary range: $21,000 to $24,000
Prerequisites: Bachelor's degree
Employers: The government, retail stores, car dealerships, restaurants, etc.
Websites for Review: www.napm.org (Institute for Supply Management) www.nigp.org (National Institute of Governmental Purchasing, Inc.)

A purchasing manager can best be described as a bargain shopper searching for the best price on products his or her company will sell. He or she can negotiate with the wholesaler in order to get the best price. In large corporations, purchasing managers buy in enormous quantities and are able to experience economies of scale. Economies of scale can be explained as the lowering of unit costs due to the purchase of such a high volume of units. This allows them to keep their prices low, which ultimately is good for the consumer.

In order to make a good purchasing decision, purchasing agents must be completely knowledgeable of the products they buy. Most purchasing managers will specialize in one area. Companies that have several departments, such as Wal-Mart, will hire several purchasing managers. This will ensure they can focus on their own line of products.

Disadvantages

The use of computers has simplified this position. However, as a purchasing manager of a large company, such as Wal-Mart, you can imagine how complex the purchasing system can be. In a Super Wal-Mart, you can find everything from food to car accessories.

Purchasing managers work in a fast-paced environment that may be stressful at times. During busy seasons, some purchasing managers may be required to work more than the typical 40-hour week, including evenings and weekends. There may also be hours that will be spent on the road traveling to trade shows where wholesalers present their products.

Advantages

When given the opportunity to pursue a career as a purchasing manager, you will feel extremely necessary, as well as important, to the whole company. It is your job to ensure that all products are purchased and at a reasonable price. You will have the capability to spend thousands of dollars purchasing either raw materials for your company to produce a finished product or to purchase finished products at wholesale to sell at a profit. You can negotiate with the seller to get cheaper prices as well. The more your company sells a particular item, the more bargaining power you will have as a purchasing manager.

Most purchasing managers work in an office under good conditions. As decision makers for the company's purchases, they work within strict financial guideliness. But when they stay under budget, they usually find themselves rewarded with nice bonuses and other perks to keep them motivated.

HOTEL MANAGER

My dream job as a teenager was to be a hotel manager. I believed running a hotel would give me the opportunity to give guests the enjoyment of their life. Providing thrills and excitement and little surprises in a guest's stay with your hotel is what can make you feel good about your job. As an alumni cast member of the Walt Disney World Corporation in Orlando, Florida, I was introduced to the concept of putting your guests first.

CAREER PROFILE
Entry salary range: $28,000 to $33,000
Prerequisites: Associate degree or sufficient experience
Employers: Almost all hotels, motels, and resorts across the United States
Websites for Review: www.ieha.org (International Executive Housekeepers Association) www.ei-ahma.org (Educational Institute of the American Hotel and Motel Association)

There are several different types of managers in a hotel—resident manager, front office managers, housekeeping managers, and others. Typically, you will begin your career in hotel management as an assistant manager. There are several assistant managers within each hotel who take care of phone calls, small problems, and most importantly, the happiness of the guests.

Hotels, motels, and resorts are all different sizes and can occupy different numbers of people. For convenience, I will be discussing a hotel that consists of approximately 400 rooms, several employees, and has many positions available in management.

The resident manager is typically an eight-to-five employee but is always on call. They generally live in the hotel in case something serious happens and needs to be taken care of quickly. The resident manager is one who looks over the entire hotel. He or she will set the rates for the rooms given certain guidelines. If a television, heater, air conditioner, or any other appliance needs to be replaced, the general manager must be the one who approves this action. Some resident managers will even consider their hotel as their baby and they must protect it at all costs.

The front office manager is just that, the manager of the front office. The front office acts almost like a separate entity in that they take care of reservations, money, and telephone calls. Also, this is where complaints are made, so it is the front office manager who will take care of most of the problems, unless they are serious, in which case the resident manager will be called.

The housekeeping manager is responsible for ensuring that all guest rooms, banquet rooms, workout rooms, and other general locations of the hotel are kept clean. If you have ever had the opportunity to stay in a hotel, the housekeeping manager was the person to oversee the housekeepers who came to your room and provided fresh towels, made your beds, and vacuumed the floors. Generally, the housekeeping manager will have a lot of guest interaction throughout the entire hotel so it is crucial that he or she have knowledge of the entire hotel and its operations.

Disadvantages

The biggest disadvantage is dealing with complaints. With a hotel consisting of 400 rooms, things go wrong on a daily basis. It is tough trying to keep up with everything and ensure that you are making each guest feel equally as important as the next. It is your job to ensure that each and every problem is not just taken care of, but that it is done in a timely manner.

Also, if you are a manager in the off-season of tourism, you may find yourself with nothing to do. In Panama City Beach, Florida, the winters are nearly like a ghost town. There are few guests to attend to and your days may seem long. On the other hand, when you are in the middle of the tourist season, some days may seem so hectic you cannot keep up with your daily activities. Although there are boring times and busy times, ensuring that each guest is well taken care of will ensure repeat customers. That is the most crucial part of your business.

The general manager, who is on call at all times, may have to work odd hours or even be distracted during his or her free time. This may be a big disadvantage to those who have families and do not want to leave them to attend to a guest's problems.

Advantages

Being a hotel manager gives you the opportunity to make each guest's stay fun and relaxing. Many people take just one trip each year and during that trip they do not want to worry about anything. This automatically makes everything they do not want to do, your job. Seeing the smile on your guests' faces is rewarding. To some hotel managers, their job is kind of like being a hero. This is the chance for people to leave reality and enter a world of imagination. The hotel manager has the opportunity to create a luxury world to ensure that the guests will be back next year and the year after that. As the resident manager, you are generally given a place to live free of charge. Therefore, you are expected to be on call at all times.

RESTAURANT MANAGER

Imagine you are the manager of the hottest restaurant in town. For the hour or so your patrons are in your restaurant, you have the ability to make their time enjoyable and well worth the money they are paying. You who will be responsible if there are any problems that should arise. It is you the people will complain to so it is your hard work and dedication to your restaurant that will either make people come back again or not.

CAREER PROFILE
Entry salary range: $23,000 to $25,500
Prerequisites: Associate degree or sufficient experience
Employers: All restaurants
Websites for Review: www.edfound.org (National Restaurant Association Educational Foundation)   http://chrie.org (Council on Hotel, Restaurant, and Institutional Education)

Restaurant managers are responsible for all aspects of their restaurant. They must be comfortable with the interviewing, hiring, and firing of their employees. They must self-motivate plus motivate their employees to ensure they are doing the best job they can. Generally, the restaurant manager will have several assistant managers who work odd shifts to run the restaurant when the manager cannot be there. The assistant manager acts in place of the manager when problems with customers or employees occur.

Restaurant managers are also responsible for ordering fresh foods, cooking supplies, and eating utensils to maintain the restaurant. Through training and experience with foods, the restaurant must distinguish between fresh foods and foods that cannot be served.

Complying with the government is crucial when it comes to the cleanliness of the restaurant. This includes the dining room, kitchen, bathrooms, and all other rooms. If an inspector feels a restaurant is dirty, it can be completely shut down until the problem is remedied.

Disadvantages

As a restaurant manager, it is your job to ensure that everything is run properly because if it is not, it will come back to you. When food is not prepared correctly or is served spoiled, lawsuits can be filed and you can lose your job. Ensuring that only the finest foods are served is a main priority for the restaurant manager. Also, odd hours, such as weekends and evenings, may be mandatory. If you experience an assistant manager who decides to quit without notice, it is your job to cover that shift no matter how many hours you have put in for the week.

When customers are complaining about the service, employees are grumbling about work conditions, the cook is worried about being underpaid, and you are on your 12th straight hour of work with no breaks, you may find your stress level reaching an all-time high. It is your duty to keep everything under control.

Advantages

Although you are supplying a product, the service you provide is what makes a restaurant impressive or just another restaurant. It is your job to give your customers the best experience possible. The service a customer receives will leave a much bigger impact than the food they eat.

As a manager, almost everything that happens to the restaurant is accredited to you. The harder you work at making the customer's experience pleasant and enjoyable, the better the reputation you will earn. Although there are a lot of responsibilities attached, when you become good at what you do, a career as a restaurant manager can be one of the most rewarding.

Successful Interviewing

In order to be a successful interviewee, one must understand why he or she is going to the interview. The purpose of the interview is not for you to determine if this is the job of your dreams. The interview will give you a chance to ask questions and find out if this is a job that you would like. Also, the interview will enable the employer to select an individual who best fits the qualifications and profile wanted for the position.

Your appearance is important so make sure you are well groomed. If you look sloppy, an interviewer might assume your performance on the job will be sloppy. Your values and goals for the future are also important. If you are an outgoing individual and can display this energy to the interviewer, you are already competing well at this game. The interviewer wants to know whether or not you will excel in the company's corporate culture and if there is a possible future in a higher position for you. Basically, they want to know how much you will benefit the company's long- and short-term goals. Long-term prospects for employees are important to a company. Most companies want to hire an individual who is interested in staying with the company long-term and is going to benefit the company way down the road.

To get yourself in the door, there are many techniques that you are already aware of, the most effective of which is networking. This is a sure way of letting the employer know you are interested in the job that has been posted. Using employment services and answering ads are also ways to get interviews. I have combined internships, networking, and sending out my resume to get my name out to prospective employers. Use your resume as a tool to show prospective employers what you have done during your years in school and what you are capable of now.

The Internet has increased the visibility of jobs, but it has also increased the competition between prospective employees. Some helpful websites are www.monster.com, www.headhunter.net, and www.hotjobs.com. On all three of these websites you have the ability to search for jobs, post your resume for employers to find you, and research companies you would like to know more about.

Interviewing for a job is the most crucial part of earning you a good career. As many people will tell you, interviewing is just like any other thing you do. The more experience you have, the better you will perform under pressure. Do not be discouraged if the first few interviews do not go as well as you expect. It is a tough market and while one may think they can walk in unemployed and walk out with a new job, it's usually not that easy.

Marketing and Advertising

CHAPTER 5

MARKETING MANAGER

One of the main goals for any corporation or large company is to gain as much market share as possible. It is crucial for the survival of any company to establish this market share and then maintain it for as long as they plan to hold on to their product line. It is up to the marketing manager to determine the liquidity of a certain product or product line to determine if the product will sell quickly or not. It is crucial for every company that plans to stay in existence to have a marketing manager who understands the business and is effective and efficient at reaching the company's long-term goals.

One of the more basic tasks of the marketing manager is to take all of the information collected by a marketing research analyst and put it to work. With this information, they can determine which products are going to be profitable and which should be cut out of the product line. Also, the marketing manager must determine the demand of the product so a price can be set to maximize profits. All of the planning of a prod-

CAREER PROFILE
Entry salary range: $19,000 to $24,000
Pre-requisites: MBA is preferred but a bachelor's degree is acceptable when beginning at the bottom
Employers: Car dealerships, entertainment corporations, retail stores, travel destinations
Websites for Review: www.marketingpower.com (American Marketing Association) www.smei.org (Sales and Marketing Executives International, Inc,)

uct, such as the development, promotion, and distribution, weighs heavily on the mind of the marketing manager. Should a company distribute overseas or should it remain a domestic company only? This is just one of the many questions faced by the marketing manager.

It is obvious one individual cannot do all of this work alone. The marketing manager will have several assistants to help tackle the major areas of the marketing of a product. It is essential that the marketing manager knows how to deal with people and is an experienced team leader. It is the marketing manager who spends most of his or her time getting others to do the work. The marketing manager could also be considered the marketing coordinator. A good marketing manager must communicate well with everyone. If communication is poor between the marketing manager and the assistants, problems may arise. Marketing managers must plan well and be flexible to adapt to any situations that come up.

A marketing manager will also face several deadlines before a product is shipped to be sold. The marketing manager must ensure that their assistants

MARKETING AND ADVERTISING

accomplish all of the steps that must be done to get the product out onto the sales floor.

Disadvantages

Marketing managers usually work in stressful, fast-paced environments. From the beginning of the research process to the distribution of the product, the marketing manager must stay on top of the planning process to ensure the product is available at the right time. Consider a popular toy that must be available in stores for Christmas. It is marketing strategy alone that will ensure the toys are released at the perfect time.

An individual does not simply graduate from college with a bachelor's degree and jump right in to a job as a marketing manager. Individuals who want to pursue this career will find themselves at the bottom working their way up to assistant and then to marketing manager.

As with most careers, the more education you have, the more likely you will advance into this career. It is expected that by the time that you acquire enough experience in the marketing field, an MBA will also be acquired. Having an MBA and sufficient experience will increase your chances of finding a career in this arena.

Advantages

If you love to talk and form relationships with people, this might be the career you are looking for. More than 50 percent of your time as a marketing manager will be spent talking to your assistants and to other individuals who play parts in getting your product to the public. The feeling of fulfillment when your product hits the shelf in the local grocery or department store is probably the greatest reward to this career because the work that it takes to get there is immeasurable.

In recent years, companies have discovered that a great deal of research can pay off tremendously. With this discovery comes a greater expansion of this career. In particular, when dealing with companies in the technology sector or the health sector, research is crucial to the career of a marketing manager.

ASSISTANT ADVERTISING AGENT

Many people agree that the best part of the Super Bowl is the commercials. These advertisements are the cream of the crop. They combine experience, creativity, and a huge imagination to tell the world why their product is the right choice for the consumer. It is the assistant advertising agent's job to create, as well as structure, advertisements that appeal to the consumer. Commercials during the Super Bowl are not only more creative, but the budgets are high. An advertising agent is required to be artistic and creative.

CAREER PROFILE
Entry salary range: $24,000 to $29,000
Prerequisites: Bachelor's degree
Employers: Independent marketing companies, manufacturing firms, web-based businesses, etc.
Websites for Review: www.af.org/pub/aaf/ (American Advertising Federation)   http://nsns.com/mix/ (American Marketing Association)

Working as an advertising agent is one of the most stressful jobs in the marketing and advertising world. They deal with many problems that can arise 10 minutes before deadline. Communication skills are so crucial in this career that speaking in front of small or large groups must become second nature in your daily work. PowerPoint and other software will be used frequently for client presentations. The ability to work with fellow employees in a team setting, accuracy, and paying close attention to the details of a project are also important.

As the assistant advertising agent, you will be aided by many other employees within your firm. The consumers will not see most of your work. One of your main goals is to ensure that your firm is staying within the budgeted price you and your client set for the project. Once your creative team has come together and produced exactly what your client is looking for, it is your opportunity to present your finished product to them. Once the client approves the finished product, you and your team will go into the actual production. Production can take anywhere from a few days or in the case of a large project, several months.

Disadvantages

If this is the line of work you feel best suits your personality, you must be willing to accept a job in a larger city such as Los Angeles, Chicago, Atlanta, or New York. Finding a job in this field around your local town may turn out to be an impossible task. Also, once you get to a larger city where the opportunity does exist, these jobs do not just become available right away. They are tough to get into right out of college so starting at the bottom and working your way up is something that must be accepted before deciding on your future. If you do find a job in a smaller city, the advancement and salary will not compare to that of a larger city.

Accepting a fast-paced career with many deadlines is essential to your future as an assistant advertising agent. Also, to add to the stress, you will be expected to tackle several tasks at once. If a hectic lifestyle is not for, search elsewhere for a career.

Advantages

If your personality fits the needs of this career, you will find it rewarding. Using your creativity, imagination, and intelligence in handling personal relationships will make you a hero to a lot of companies just starting out or offering a new product line. If you become good at your job and understand what makes a good advertising agent, you will find yourself meeting some important people while making an impressive salary. It is not uncommon for an advertising agent to be making a six-figure salary.

Individuals who find this line of work to be appealing will be able to display their energy and creative talents in ways they never thought possible. This is their chance to show the world what they are made of and to convince people their ideas and thoughts are better than the next person's. Energy flows through the office in the form of creativity, excitement, and deadlines.

JUNIOR MARKETING RESEARCH ANALYST

Junior marketing research analysts are generally working their way up to become a marketing research analyst. They will find themselves being supervised by the marketing research analyst and performing some of the same duties. The role of the marketing research analyst can be a lot of fun. It involves collecting information using a collectively exhaustive questionnaire, interviewing individuals, or monitoring the activities of consumers through other available sources of data. This information is then gathered up and analyzed so products and services can be designed to fit the consumer's needs. Basically, they try to find what will make more customers purchase their product. Without the marketing research analyst, there would be a lot of useless products.

CAREER PROFILE
Entry salary range: $22,000 to $27,000
Prerequisites: Bachelor's degree
Employers: Entertainment industry, car manufacturers, food manufacturers, clothing designers
Websites for Review: http://nsns.com/mix (American Marketing Association) www.commercepark.com/AAAA/AAAA.html (American Association of Advertising Agencies)

Have you ever been sitting at home when the phone rings and the person on the other end just wants to ask you a couple of questions? Maybe you have been walking down the mall when you see the people with the clipboards. These individuals are trying to collect the necessary data to make our lives better through the use of products. After all of this information is collected, the marketing research analysts will put it into charts and other readable forms so that better sense may be made of it.

Why is the role of the marketing research analyst important to firms? The firm can then analyze the data gathered and make better decisions on what to produce, how to produce it, and how to display it so that it will come across as a much better product than their competitor's. Making a good product with good quality is important but if no one wants to purchase it, what good is it to the consumers?

The marketing research analyst should be comfortable with computers. They will use a lot of different software to compile data-making charts and other readable graphs so materials can be analyzed. Also, computers are being used as a source for collecting information. Questionnaires as well as monitoring how many times a certain link to another website is clicked on are other ways that research is taking place. Computers are smart enough now that when you log on to a website, it will monitor every place that you click on. Some think of this as an invasion of privacy, but others know it will give companies a better understanding of how consumers think allowing them to shape their products to better fit the consumers' wants and needs.

Also important to the outcome of good, accurate, and reliable research is the analyst's ability to communicate well. It is important for the analyst to have good communication skills because, if you communicate badly, your data will come back contaminated. Having the ability to get your point across to the consumers will ensure they give you accurate data.

Disadvantages

The marketing research analysts will find themselves under a lot of time deadlines. Their work will be consumed with a lot of alone time working to prepare data so that the firm's decision-making team can read it. The marketing research analyst will be expected to work overtime in the event that a deadline is approaching or if the firm is expanding into other markets. It is the chore of the analyst to determine just how the company should go about the new venture into new markets.

Most consumers will not want to take the time out of their daily lives to talk to you. A lot of times people will get upset or hang up on you. If you are in the mall with a clipboard, people will walk on the other side of the mall just to avoid you. It is tough to always get the information you need from consumers but it is imperative that you do, in order to make good decisions for your firm.

Advantages

For individuals who need to see accomplishments in their work, this career might be right for you. Imagine your boss coming to you and saying that the board of directors has decided to move into a new market. The company now needs for you to conduct research so they can accurately make the correct decisions concerning this product. After you collect these data you find there is a niche market and you can differentiate your product in a certain way that will fit the consumer's needs better than what is currently being offered. With completion of the study, your company jumps on the bandwagon and decides to supply 250,000 units of this product to consumers. When the product hits the streets it is popular. Your company has now increased its market share with this new product line. The patent of this new product, your information, and hard work are what made this all possible.

DESIGNER

There is a vast amount of material available on designers. Designers are everywhere. They design clothes, cars, homes, offices, gardens, tools, bicycles, stuffed animals, cartoons, and so forth. Designers are needed in almost every business provided their business produces some sort of output. (I have dedicated one section of this book in the first chapter to web-page design.)

CAREER PROFILE
Entry salary range: $18,000 to $22,000
Prerequisites: Bachelor's degree
Employers: Automobile manufacturers, clothes manufacturers, computer companies
Websites for Review: www.idsa.org (Industrial Designers Society of America) www.aiga.org (American Institute of Graphic Arts)

For the next few pages, I will be referring to designers of cars, clothing, and other companies that require a secondary education. Most interior decorators or floral design companies do not require a college degree.

A designer loves to create. It is crucial that you, as a designer, have an artistic mind with an imagination to dream up new ideas. Most car companies will have one room in which designers will sit at a computer all day and dream up innovative body styles for their new cars. This process of dreaming goes on until the right body style is found.

Clothing designers will spend endless hours coming up with new fashion trends for the upcoming year. The new dress, the new bikini, or the new mini-skirt are all responsibilities of the clothing designers. If they do not have the new style for the next year, their company will lose a lot of their market share and it will be the designer's responsibility.

Disadvantages

There is a lot of pressure that can be put on a designer due to the deadlines that must be met. Just as an author of a book, there are some days that you sit down to write, and nothing comes out. Imagine having a deadline of one week and every day you sit down and nothing comes out. You sit, play, and try to come up with something that only leads you to more frustration. When these blocks occur, working evenings, weekends, and even holidays are mandatory to meet deadlines.

Advantages

Imagine a job that allows you to sit in front of a computer and dream up the impossible, then make it possible. Or running simulations and testing models out on a computer to see if the technology of today will fit your imagination of tomorrow. Imagine working for Ford Motor Company and it is your creation that has been selected for this year's new Mustang. When the first model hits the street and everyone loves this car, you are responsible. This happens to someone every year for every car company for every model.

Good Luck!

As you begin to find your way through life, you will find that there are many different interests that satisfy your needs. By reading this book, I hope that you have been able to take bits and pieces from each area to help you better understand that you are going to experience many changes throughout your life. Jobs may come and go. The key is to always try to make yourself a little bit better than you were before you began the job.

Whatever it is that you pursue throughout your life, I wish you luck. Explore the unexplored and remember what you have already explored. Keep an open mind about your future and simply enjoy the ride.

BIBLIOGRAPHY

Bloch, Deborah P. *How to Have a Winning Job Interview.* 3rd ed. Lincolnwood, Illinois: NTC Publishing Group, 1998.

———. *How to Write a Winning Resume.* 4th ed. Lincolnwood, Illinois: NTC Publishing Group, 1998.

Professional & Technical Careers: a Guide from World Book. Chicago, Illinois: World Book, Inc., 1998.

Burnett, Rebecca. *Careers for Number Crunchers & Other Quantitative Types.* 2nd ed. New York City, New York: The McGraw-Hill Companies, 2002.

Camenson, Blythe. *Real People Working in Finance.* Lincolnwood, Illinois: NTC Publishing Group, 1999.

———. *Real People Working in Sales & Marketing.* Lincolnwood, Illinois: NTC Publishing Group, 1997.

Eberts, Marjorie and Margaret Gisler. *Careers for Financial Mavens & Other Money Movers.* Lincolnwood, Illinois: NTC Publishing Group, 1999.

The Editors of VGM Career Horizons. *VGM's Careers Encyclopedia.* Lincolnwood, Illinois: NTC Publishing Group, 1997.

Farr, J. Michael. *America's Fastest Growing Jobs.* 6th ed. Indianapolis, Indiana: JIST Works, Inc., 2001.

———. *America's Top Jobs for College Graduates*. 3d ed. Indianapolis, Indiana: JIST Works, Inc.,1999.

———. *America's Top Office Management, Sales & Professional Jobs*. Indianapolis, Indiana: JIST Works, Inc., 1997.

———. *America's Top White-Collar Jobs*. 5th ed. Indianapolis, Indiana: JIST Works, Inc., 2001.

——— and LaVerne L. Ludden, Ed.D. *Best Jobs for the 21st Century*. 2nd ed. Indianapolis, Indiana: JIST Works, Inc., 2001.

Fein, Richard. *100 Great Jobs and How to Get Them*. Manassas Park, Virginia: Impact Publications, 1999.

Field, Shelly. *The Unofficial Guide to Hot Careers*. Foster City, California: IDG Books Worldwide, Inc., 2000.

Fogg, Neeta P., Paul E. Harrington, and Thomas F. Harrington. *The College Majors Handbook*. Indianapolis, Indiana: JIST Works, Inc., 1999.

Gaylord, Gloria L. and Glenda E. Ried. *Careers in Accounting*. Lincolnwood, Illinois: VGM Career Horizons, 1998.

Goldberg, Jan. *Great Jobs for Accounting Majors*. Lincolnwood, Illinois: VGM Career Horizons, 1998.

———. *Great Jobs for Computer Science Majors*. Lincolnwood, Illinois: VGM Career Horizons, 1998.

Haddock, Patricia. *Careers in Banking and Finance*. New York City, New York: The Rosen Publishing Group, Inc., 1990.

Harkavy, Michael. *101 Careers*. 2nd ed. New York City, New York: John Wiley & Sons, Inc., 1999.

Hawkins, Lori and Betsy Dowling. *100 Jobs in Technology*. New York City, New York: Macmillan, 1996.

Henderson, Harry. *Career Opportunities in Computers and Cyberspace*. New York City, New York: Checkmark Books, 1999.

Phifer, Paul. *Great Careers in 2 Years*. New York City, New York: Ferguson Publishing Company, 2000.

Stair, Lila B. *Careers In Business*. Lincolnwood, Illinois: VGM Career Horizons, 1998.

——— and Leslie Stair. *Careers in Marketing*. 3d ed. New York City, New York: The McGraw-Hill Companies, 2002.

Wright, John W. *The American Almanac of Jobs and Salaries*. New York City, New York: Avon Books, 1996.

ABOUT THE AUTHOR

M. J. Giles holds a bachelor's degree in finance from the University of Southern Indiana School of Business. A recent graduate, he made it his mission to become familiar with the multitude of business career opportunities while still a student. During college Giles held three business internships and two professional work stints in the financial, investment, and accounting fields, along with serving as president of the student Economics and Finance Club and Investment Club. Giles currently lives and works in Evansville, Indiana, and is employed by ONB Investment Services, Inc., as a registered brokerage operations specialist.

INDEX

N

P

Q

R

S

Give the Gift of

Young Adult's Guide
to a Business Career

to Your Friends and Colleagues

CHECK YOUR LEADING BOOKSTORE
OR ORDER FROM:

BookMasters Distribution Center
30 Amberwood Pkwy.
Ashland, OH 44805

(800) 247-6553—Toll free book order #

(419) 281-1802—International phone #

(419) 281-6883—Fax #

order@bookmaster.com—email order address